# NORFOLK'S RAILWAYS

## Volume 2: The Midland & Great Northern Joint Railway

A Portrait in Old Picture Postcards

by

Mike Handscomb and Philip Standley

S. B. Publications

1992

By the same authors:
*Norfolk's Railways, Volume 1: G.E.R., A Portrait in Old Picture Postcards.*

First published in 1992 by S. B. Publications

Unit 2, The Old Station Yard,
Pipe Gate, Market Drayton, Shropshire TF9 4HY.

ISBN 1 85770 010 4

Typeset and printed by Geo. R. Reeve Ltd., Wymondham, Norfolk NR18 0BD.

# CONTENTS

*Front Cover:* Goods train at Drayton

# INTRODUCTION

February 28th 1959: Norwich City fans were celebrating their team's heroic 1-1 draw against Sheffield United in the sixth round of the F.A.Cup. But in towns and villages right across Norfolk there was little cause for cheer, for that day British Railways ran its very last trains on the Midland & Great Northern line. Short stretches were still to see trains, mostly freight, for a few more years, but as an entity the M&GN — loved, derided, taken for granted and passed between a succession of owners — was gone forever.

It had begun in a remarkably piecemeal fashion. A number of local companies were formed in the 1850s onwards to bring railways to tracts of agricultural Norfolk and Lincolnshire which either had none or were at the mercy of the Great Eastern Railway. Names such as 'The Lynn and Sutton Bridge' or 'The Great Yarmouth and Stalham' indicated their initial plans but not necessarily their more grandiose long-term goals. They made alliances and working agreements, usually in conjunction with or encouraged by the Midland Railway and the Great Northern, both of whom stood to benefit from through traffic to and from Norfolk. In 1893 the MR and GNR succeeded in buying the last of the local concerns, which had become saddled by debt, and as a result they now owned a continuous route stretching from their own systems right over to Yarmouth, with branches to Norwich and Cromer for good measure. Each company appointed directors to run the line and thus the Midland & Great Northern Railways Joint Committee —'the Joint'— was born.

There followed a period of prosperity which is reflected in many of the scenes illustrated here. Tracks were doubled, or equipped with automatic tablet-exchangers, to speed up trains. New engines arrived and more long-distance expresses were introduced. For many, the epitome of the line was the sight of a smart yellow 4-4-0 running at speed on the 'Leicester', a popular and long-lived service which despite its nickname ran through to Birmingham.

The sequence of views in this book, like Volume 1, represents a series of journeys during the first two or three decades of this century. Entering Norfolk from the west, we take the main line through South Lynn, Fakenham, Melton Constable and North Walsham to Yarmouth. Then from Melton we proceed in turn to Norwich and Cromer. Also illustrated are the coastal routes which were a joint venture between the M&GN and the GER: North Walsham to Cromer via Mundesley, and Yarmouth to Lowestoft. The body set up to run these lines revelled in the title of the Norfolk & Suffolk Joint Railways Committee.

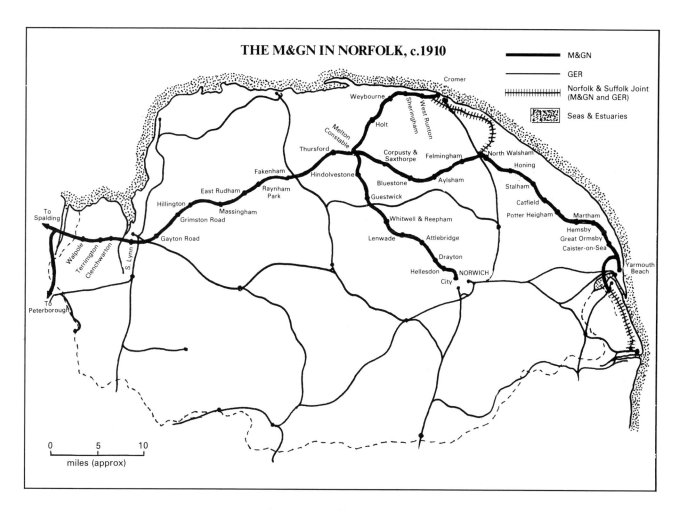

# THE M&GN IN NORFOLK, c.1910

M&GN
GER
Norfolk & Suffolk Joint (M&GN and GER)
Seas & Estuaries

Cromer
Weybourne
Sheringham
West Runton
Holt
Melton Constable
Thursford
Corpusty & Saxthorpe
Felmingham
North Walsham
Honing
Fakenham
Hindolvestone
Bluestone
Aylsham
Stalham
Raynham Park
Guestwick
Catfield
East Rudham
Potter Heigham
Martham
Hillington
Massingham
Whitwell & Reepham
Grimston Road
Hemsby
Great Ormsby
Caister-on-Sea
Gayton Road
Lenwade
Attlebridge
To Spalding
S. Lynn
Walpole
Terrington
Clenchwarton
Drayton
Hellesdon
NORWICH City
Yarmouth Beach
To Peterborough

0   5   10
miles (approx)

# INTRODUCTION (Continued)

Though its offices were at King's Lynn the M&GN's heart lay at Melton Constable. This tiny village underwent an astonishing transformation into a major railway centre. From its busy station trains departed in four directions, and right alongside were the line's locomotive and rolling-stock workshops. Supervising all engineering matters, and also Traffic Manager by the end of his 43-year career on the line, was a man who appears several times in these pages. William Marriott's name was virtually synonymous with the Joint, and much of its efficient operation was credited to him.

In 1936 came a watershed. The M&GN had become the joint property of the LMS and the LNER, and they agreed that the latter should take sole charge of operating it. Without delay Melton Constable locomotive works closed (repairs were transferred to Stratford) and a large centre of employment vanished. M&GN locomotives were replaced by other LNER types and the Joint's individuality began an irrevocable decline.

The strategic importance of East Anglian airfields meant that the Joint played its full part in World War 2. After the War, and with the railways now nationalized, its holiday expresses were as popular as ever; but with much of its route duplicated by ex-GER lines and more and more traffic switching to the roads, British Railways' Eastern Region management became convinced that closing it would bring large savings. Indeed many believe it was deliberately starved of traffic to make the case for closure more overwhelming.

Thus on that February evening in 1959 crowds turned out for the last train and Norfolk's railway map lost its principal east-west route at a stroke. Today only the Cromer — Sheringham portion carries BR trains, but westwards out of Sheringham the North Norfolk Railway, or 'Poppy Line' as it likes to be known, still operates steam trips over five miles of the old line. Around the county too, the Joint's old stations and crossing-keepers' cottages may still be discovered. Some are little changed from these postcard views and others rather more down-at-heel, but each is a reminder of a railway which unassumingly served Norfolk farmers, holidaymakers, servicemen and schoolchildren for many years and is still remembered with affection.

## 1. ACROSS NORTH—WEST NORFOLK

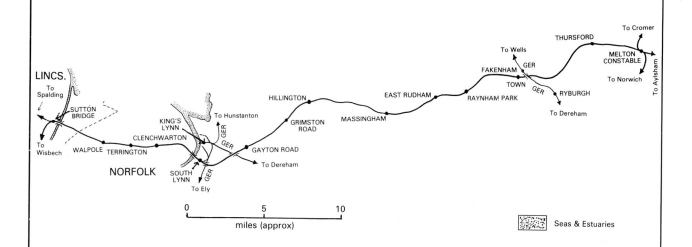

miles (approx)

Seas & Estuaries

The Lynn & Sutton Bridge Railway, opened in 1866, was the first Norfolk element of what was to become the M&GN. Fourteen years later the Lynn & Fakenham Company connected the two towns of its title (and then pushed on past Melton Constable to Norwich). Through trains once had to reverse at the rival GER's Lynn station, but the 1886 avoiding line known as the Bawsey loop eliminated this procedure. The South Lynn - East Rudham portion survived the 1959 closure; grain was despatched from East Rudham along the line until 1968.

Sutton Bridge752.

**CROSS KEYS BRIDGE**

A C class 4-4-0 draws its train over Cross Keys bridge and into Sutton Bridge station. Although 1½ miles inside Lincolnshire this swing bridge over the River Nene was the M&GN's effective gateway to Norfolk. It was opened in 1897 and had adjacent spans for road and rail traffic - a great improvement on the previous bridge where the two had shared one carriageway! Shipping had priority: when a vessel approached, a large bell on the nearer signal-box was rung to warn the driver of a Norfolk-bound train standing at the station that the bridge was about to swing open and so he should cross it without delay. Refurbished at a cost of £2.8m, the bridge now carries the important A17 road.

## WALPOLE STATION

Five minutes away from Sutton Bridge was Walpole. The signals and signal-box visible here were, like all those on the Lynn & Sutton Bridge line, of Midland Railway design. In the fruit season the sidings here and down the line would be crammed with ventilated box vans, and cart after cart would drive up with produce to be loaded. Twenty years after the railway's closure the A17 road was re-routed along it between the rivers Nene and Ouse, and the remains of Walpole, Terrington and Clenchwarton stations were swept away.

**CLENCHWARTON STATION**

Whitewashed stones were often arranged to spell out a M&GN station's name. At the base of these attractive foliage-covered buildings the three nearest panels read CLENCH WARTON M&GN. A celebration appears to be taking place, for a Union Jack has been hoisted aloft, two smaller ones hang from the house, and what could be a home-made banner flutters above a poster advertising Great Yarmouth. It is obvious how the staff travelled to and from work!

**SOUTH LYNN STATION**

This, the second South Lynn station, was built in a half-timbered style and replaced a more modest affair east of Saddlebow Road. The track heading for the camera is the up main, unusually served by two platform faces. Over on the left is the down main and across the wooden platform is the up slow line. By the engine is a pair of GNR-type miniature somersault signals for 'wrong road' movements. Little of this busy station remains other than a siding to British Sugar's factory. Where a new asbestos-clad engine shed was erected in 1958 - a year before the line's closure! - there is now a travellers' site.

**LOCAL TRAIN AT KING'S LYNN JUNCTION**

The joint leased part of King's Lynn station from the GER and ran its own trains to and from South Lynn, using GER-owned track for most of the way. Here 0-6-0 tank no.15 hurries its ex-GNR coaches past King's Lynn Junction signal-box. The double track diverging from the train's path is the GER's Hunstanton branch, and on the extreme right is a short siding. The footbridge by the signal-box and its later replacement were useful when the gates across Tennyson Avenue were closed to road traffic for long periods. This facility has now been removed because of the erection of overhead equipment for the Cambridge - King's Lynn electrification.

**GAYTON ROAD STATION**

Tucked away among woodland and heather-covered sandhills at the east end of the Bawsey loop was Gayton Road station. The staff under stationmaster John Bacon saw few passengers; but they were dedicated gardeners and their efforts were rewarded with the 'Best Kept Station' prize several times in the 1920s and 1930s. Sidings led off from the station to sand pits operated by J. Boam & Son. The firm despatched a daily 100 tons or more of sand over the M&GN, and also used the GER's Middleton station a mile or so to the south. All that remain now are the platforms, half hidden in undergrowth near the Sand Boy Inn.

Hillington Station.    J 5280.    (Hardy's Series.)

## HILLINGTON STATION

An attractive pavilion-style brick building with twin gables characterized many M&GN stations. Here on Hillington's up platform is the first of them, built in 1879. Though 'Hillington for Sandringham' boasted special waiting rooms kept in readiness, royalty preferred to patronize the GER at Wolferton with its easier access to London. Behind stationmaster Mr Drayton and the passengers awaiting a down train is the signal-box which was later moved up to the road crossing so that it could operate the gates as well. The up side buildings became overflow accommodation for the village school in the 1960s. They have since been converted into a house, and a row of tall conifers obscures this view from the road.

**ACCIDENT AT HILLINGTON**

This unfortunate episode occured in March 1909. A train of wagons was standing at the down platform while a horse was being unloaded. 4-4-0 no.76 approached from the Massingham direction with a goods train to Lynn. The points were set in error for the down line and no.76 ploughed into the wagons, demolishing a GER horse box and scattering wreckage over the tracks.

### MASSINGHAM STATION

A driving force behind the building of the Lynn & Fakenham line was Revd. Joseph Brereton of Little Massingham, and supporters of the project used to meet at his rectory in the 1870s. This view of Revd. Brereton's local station was taken some thirty years after the trains first ran, and a prominent feature is the criss-cross fencing which was once to be found all over the M&GN. Massingham was the only station between South Lynn and Fakenham to be favoured with a footbridge. The main building and the stationmaster's house beside it are both now occupied as private houses.

**RAYNHAM PARK STATION**

A more apposite name for this station would have been Helhoughton; but the Lynn & Fakenham's chairman was Marquis Townshend of Raynham Hall (a descendant of the agricultural innovator 'Turnip' Townshend) and doubtless his views on what to call the station held sway! This idyllic scene, with two open tourers parked outside the station entrance, dates from about 1930. The station's present owners take pride in its history; they have maintained it much as it was and enlivened its walls with railway signs and enamel advertisements.

**FAKENHAM TOWN STATION**

With the railway's arrival in 1880, Fakenham was less than an hour from Lynn by fast train. The station's official name was Fakenham Town, but it was some way from the centre and locals knew it as Hempton as it was in that parish. Market day (Thursday) could see as many as seventy cattle wagons loaded, and race days also brought a lot of business. Signalman in the East box, on the left of the picture, was Mr. Joyce. He used to teach signalling to young railway clerks during their lunch hour. The station site is now a Jewson's building supplies depot. By the exit there is still a length of the down platform where an inconspicuous plaque records that this was once the L&FR's terminus.

Thursford Station. J 4930. (Mitchell's Series.)

## THURSFORD STATION

Looking at the site today - buildings gone, the B1354 road running along the line, council vehicles parked in the old yard - it's hard to imagine the activity when more sugar beet was loaded at Thursford than at any other M&GN station in Norfolk. From the farms it reached the station behind traction engines belonging to George Cushing, who was later to establish the Thursford Collection of steam-age bygones. Typical M&GN features portrayed here include the crossing gates with their triangular warning panels (other companies preferred discs) and lamps mounted on spikes for visibility; and the tariff shed on the up platform, a temporary storage facility for small consignments of goods.

**TRAIN AT THURSFORD**

With no engine visible at the far end, it seems that the carriages from which the elegantly-attired lady passengers are alighting on to the up platform have just pulled in *towards* the camera. Perhaps the down line was already occupied or under repair. The train is formed of ex-GNR six-wheeled stock, the nearest vehicle being a luggage van. In the early years of the century railways were still a novelty in some parts of Norfolk. George Cushing recalls how people would stroll from Hindringham and other villages on a Sunday evening just to watch the trains at Thursford.

*Midland Express nearing Melton Constable.*

**MIDLAND EXPRESS NEARING MELTON CONSTABLE**

C class 4-4-0 no.75 sweeps down the 1 in 100 bank to Melton Constable at the head of an eight-coach express. A mile back it has breasted Piggs Grave summit, the M&GN's highest point, 312 feet above sea level. Heavy trains leaving in the opposite direction often needed a banking engine to assist them as far as the advanced starting signal seen here. The permanent way looks immaculate and the milepost (pre-dating the more familiar concrete type) has received a fresh coat of paint.

**WILLIAM MARRIOTT**

William Marriott retired in 1924 after a long career supervising many of the M&GN's activities from his Melton Constable base. Named after him are Thorpe Marriott, a modern housing development near Drayton, and Marriott's Way, a long-distance footpath which Norfolk County Council has created along part of the old line to Norwich.

## 2.  MELTON CONSTABLE

From a village of around a hundred souls to Norfolk's principal railway workshop - and now a community miles from the railway; such has been Melton Constable's eventful history. Today's visitor can trace several legacies of the past: terraces of railwaymen's brick houses, out of context in the Norfolk countryside; remnants of the engineering shops, now a light industrial hotch-potch; and, brooding over the whole scene, a massive water tank with M&GN cast into every panel.

**PASSENGER TRAIN PASSING WEST BOX**

At the head of a train of Midland express stock, the majority with clerestory roofs, 4-4-0 no.3 runs into the station past Melton West box and a platelayer's trolley which has been left between the tracks. At this point the up and down lines splayed out so as to pass either side of the island platform. Crossing the train's path in the right foreground is the line to Cromer. The five-bracket headlamp arrangement on No.3 dates the photograph as taken between 1895 and 1903.

**4-4-0 AND TRAIN AT DOWN PLATFORM**

The road bridge over the line, from which passengers went down a covered stairway to the platforms, was a favourite vantage point for photographers. Here we look across the goods yard to see a Beyer Peacock 4-4-0 on an up train of mixed MR and GNR stock. Although this was nominally the down (i.e. to Yarmouth or Norwich) platform, uneven traffic flows caused both tracks to be worked in either direction and two trains sometimes occupied the same platform - hence the signs beneath the canopy directing passengers not just to No.1 or No.2 platform but to the east or west end of it as well. The bookstall at the extreme right had the odd distinction of continuing to open after the rest of the station closed in 1964.

**VIEW ALONG UP PLATFORM**

Despite the congestion at this busy junction, no up relief road was ever built and this view shows why: blocking the way was the short platform, complete with its own waiting-room, which was provided for Lord Hastings' use. Earlier cards show the waiting-room block near the camera as a rustic brick-and-timber structure, but here it has been faced with a skin of Melton Works concrete blocks. The initials CNR cast into the roof spandrels by the Ladies Waiting Room sign recall the Central Norfolk Railway. Parliament rejected its railway proposals, but a use was found for some materials which the company had already ordered.

19

**MACHINE SHOP, MELTON WORKS**

The engineering workshops occupied a ten-acre site immediately south of the station. A narrow gauge railway system conveyed heavy equipment between the various departments. The machine shop pictured here housed borers, shapers and special machines for producing copper boiler stays, while the lathes could turn anything from a bolt to a locomotive wheel (the large wheel lathe is on the right). New apprentices took a while to get used to the terrific din from the overhead shafts and drive belts.

**PERMANENT WAY GANG AT MELTON CONSTABLE**

As well as small teams of men each maintaining their own lengths of track, the M&GN had two extra gangs, based at Melton Constable and Sutton Bridge, whose job it was to re-lay and ballast track. Here the Melton gang exhibits a variety of track-laying tools under the watchful eye of foreman Mr. Strangleman.

**INSPECTION SALOON AT MELTON CONSTABLE**

Twice a year Mr Marriott and other members of the M&GN hierarchy would climb aboard this saloon and proceed to inspect the whole line. The figures lined up in this 1922 view include the resident civil engineer, the Melton Works manager and (to the right of the saloon's verandah door) Mr Marriott. In the cab of no.20A is driver Walpole. The six-wheeled saloon, 31½ feet long and dating from about 1880, was also used for judging the Best Kept Station competition.

**WITHDRAWN LOCOMOTIVES ON THE SCRAP ROAD**

Looking forlorn on the scrap siding in 1934 are rebuilt Beyer Peacock 4-4-0s nos.24 (nearest camera), 22 and 25. No.22 did not run again, but the frames of no.24 were later combined with no.25's boiler. The hybrid ran as no.025 and lasted until 1941.

RAILWAY INSTITUTE.           RAILWAY INSTITUTE.

MELTON CONSTABLE.      MELTON CONSTABLE.

### RAILWAY INSTITUTE, MELTON CONSTABLE

Two interior views of the Institute which the M&GN put up in 1896 for the staff's welfare. The billiards room was popular, but younger members were restricted to their own three-quarter-size table. In the reading room newspapers and magazines were provided and there was a large lending library. Note the locomotive portraits in each room. Other facilities included a concert hall and a restaurant. Membership cost 2d per week, a cup of cocoa 1d and a bath 2d. As Melton Constable Country Club, the building still acts as a social centre.

**LOOKING EAST FROM THE STATION**

This is what the crew of a Yarmouth express would have seen as they waited for their starter signal to drop. Behind the water column is Melton East signal-box, and just further on the tracks separate: the left-hand pair head for Yarmouth (but single track after Corpusty), and the right-hand one curves away south past sidings towards Norwich. The signal finials add distinction to the nameboard - but not so the tarpaulined spoil heap below! The tall chimney emerging from the foliage on the left belongs to the railway-owned gasworks which was built in 1899.

# 3. MELTON CONSTABLE TO THE EAST COAST

To Cromer

MELTON CONSTABLE

To Fakenham

To Norwich

CORPUSTY & SAXTHORPE

TOWN

AYLSHAM

BLUESTONE

GER

To County School

CAWSTON

FELMINGHAM

To Cromer

To Mundesley (N&S JT.)

NORTH WALSHAM TOWN

GER

GER

To Wroxham

HONING

To Wroxham

STALHAM

CATFIELD

POTTER HEIGHAM
POTTER HEIGHAM BRIDGE HALT

MARTHAM

HEMSBY

SCRATBY

GREAT ORMSBY

CALIFORNIA HALT
CAISTER CAMP HALT
CAISTER-ON-SEA
NEWTOWN HALT

GER

To Norwich

To Lowestoft (via N&S Jt.)

YARMOUTH BEACH

Seas & Estuaries

```
0          5          10
        miles (approx)
```

This 41-mile stretch was begun when the Great Yarmouth & Stalham company started laying tracks from the coast. Trains reached Stalham in 1880, North Walsham a year later. The gap between Melton Constable and North Walsham was bridged in 1883 enabling through trains to run between the Midlands and Yarmouth. Today a pleasant walk called Weavers' Way follows the route between Aylsham and Stalham. Onward to Potter Heigham the course of the railway has been turned into a road.

*Midland & G.N. Railway Bridge swept away during flood Aug 1912.*
*Corpusty    Melton & Yarmouth line*

## FLOOD DAMAGE AT THURNING

The devastation which the floods of August 1912 caused in Norfolk was well documented by photographers. Bridges and culverts on the M&GN were damaged and several landslips occurred. A mile west of Saxthorpe, close by the Thurning ballast siding, this culvert over the Blackwater stream was swept away and the rails left in the air. A more robust bridge was needed, but train services had to be restored quickly; so while it was being built the track was slewed and a temporary wooden bridge laid over the stream.

J&S 5473
N

Corpusty Station.

## CORPUSTY AND SAXTHORPE STATION

A Jarrold view taken from the road bridge and looking back to Melton Constable. From here it was single track all the way to Yarmouth. Summer Saturday trains were often held up here while they waited for clearance to enter the seven-mile section to Aylsham, and local children would wait by the line in the hope that bored holidaymakers would throw out a copper or two. Children still frequent the site, for it has become a Suffolk County Council field study centre. The building on the up (left-hand here) platform, now chimney-less, looks out over a large grassed expanse where the young visitors pitch their tents.

**STAFF AT CORPUSTY AND SAXTHORPE STATION**

This large sign was on the embankment at the Yarmouth end of the up platform, i.e. to the left of the station building in the previous picture. Keeping such signs limewashed was usually a chore delegated to the lad porter.

GYOI. MID & GT NORTHERN STATION, AYLSHAM.

## AYLSHAM TOWN STATION

In 1880 the East Norfolk Railway, soon to become part of the GER, provided Aylsham residents with their first station. Just three years later the Eastern & Midlands Railway, a constituent of the M&GN, arrived on the town's northern fringe and opened the station illustrated here. Calling it Aylsham Town could not get over the fact that it was a fair distance from the commercial centre. Regrettably nothing of this attractive station has escaped the bulldozer.

**FLOOD DAMAGE AT BANNINGHAM BRIDGE**

Along with the Thurning culvert (p. 27) this girder bridge over a north-south tributary of the Bure also succumbed to the August 1912 floods. This view shows the half-submerged remains of the brick abutments on the Felmingham side. All the M&GN's Norfolk lines were damaged to some extent but because of the collapses here and at Thurning the Melton to Yarmouth route was the last to be brought back into service.

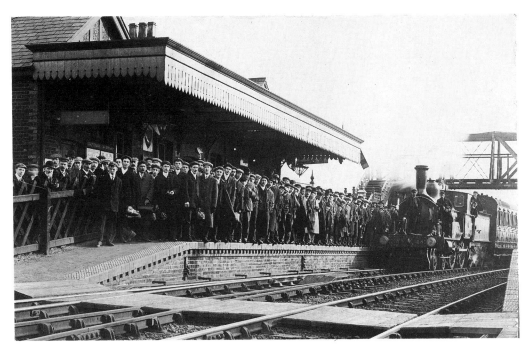

**CROWD AT NORTH WALSHAM STATION**

All eyes are on the camera as North Walsham Town football team and its supporters prepare to travel to an away fixture in about 1900. The locomotive is Beyer Peacock 4-4-0 no.28 and coupled behind it is an Eastern & Midlands third-class carriage. Trains from Aylsham passed beneath the GER's Cromer line before struggling up the 1 in 64 gradient to North Walsham station. They normally had priority over trains in the opposite direction as halting them at the foot of the gradient could be disastrous. After closure the station became a Jehovah's Witness hall but eventually disappeared to make way for the North Walsham by-pass and part of HP Foods' factory.

No. J. & S. 7329

HONING STATION.

## HONING STATION

Honing station, 'For Worstead and Dilham' according to its nameboard, was well outside the village, nearer Briggate in fact. To help keep traffic moving at busy times a half-mile long passing loop with a signal-box at each end was brought into use in 1901. With the station area now a car park for Weavers' Way walkers, only parts of the platforms and a small water-pump hut can be discovered. Honing East box was moved to the Barton House miniature railway at Wroxham, where visitors can look around it on open days.

**STALHAM STATION**

This was temporarily the terminus of the Great Yarmouth & Stalham Light Railway, but greater plans had been hatched and the light railway went on to become part of the M&GN's main line. Stalham won the Best Kept Station award in 1931 and was renowned for the roses which covered the trellis fencing. They delighted passengers and provided buttonholes for guards! The sign's claim 'For Happisburgh and Palling on Sea' makes Honing's (p.33) look restrained! The station has become a Norfolk County Council depot, and here the Stalham by-pass section of the A149 road begins. Opened in 1967, this was the first road in Norfolk to follow the line of an abandoned railway.

Station & Post Office. Potter Heigham.

84943

## POTTER HEIGHAM STATION

Potter Heigham is one of the centres for Broads holidays and the station was used by many rail-and-boat excursions until in 1933 a more convenient halt (p.37) opened right beside the river. Goods facilities at Potter Heigham were modest; the gateway just past the grass verge led to a small yard for goods and coal. The A1062 road from Ludham now joins the A149 at this spot.

**POTTER HEIGHAM RAILWAY BRIDGE**

It is said that this three-span girder bridge was built for another railway and then bought on the cheap. Whatever the truth of this, it was according to William Marriott "a local wonder" when first put up. As well as trains it carried a water main across the river Thurne. What a pity the photographer didn't wait for a 'Leicester' to trundle across! The bridge was dismantled in 1968. The road bridge which was built on its site relieved the narrow stone bridge just downstream from being choked with traffic.

**POTTER HEIGHAM BRIDGE HALT**

This was one of several small halts which the M&GN opened in 1933 as part of a determined effort to attract more holiday traffic. Platforms at all except Caister Camp Halt were at rail level and so the railcar serving them (p.43) was equipped with retractable steps. The rudimentary facilities shown here were later improved with a pair of benches for weary travellers!

Martham Station

Published by Clowes' Stores

## MARTHAM STATION

A train from Yarmouth crosses Rollesby Road as it approaches the station. There was another level crossing a little further on, which could frustrate road users when two long trains were required to pass and both gates stayed shut. In 1883 Parliament considered a proposal for a railway from Martham to Norwich. It would have created a Yarmouth - Norwich through route to compete with the GER's; but like many other schemes of the period nothing came of it. Until recently the station area was used as a bottled gas depot, and the up platform building, still with its scalloped bargeboards, acted as the depot office.

HEMSBY STATION.

## HEMSBY STATION

The line swung north of Hemsby village before curving round through the station to head due south to Ormesby. Here the photographer seems to have been captivated more by the pea crop than the station! This strip of land opposite the platform was railway property and no doubt the station staff tended it between duties. New houses, shops and the re-aligned B1159 road have obliterated most traces of the railway at Hemsby. Where the station and yard stood there is now a burial ground.

The Station, Hemsby

**HEMSBY LEVEL CROSSING**

The Street in Hemsby is temporarily obstructed while a train pauses at the station. The left-hand vehicle is an ex-GNR six-wheel third-class coach, and behind the tariff shed is a rebuilt ex-Eastern & Midlands third. It was the growing popularity and convenience of road transport, such as this splendid Queen of the Road charabanc, which prompted the M&GN to open a string of new halts at holiday camps and tourist spots in 1933.

The Station, Gt. Ormesby.

**GREAT ORMESBY STATION**

Of all the stations along the Yarmouth line, perhaps this one retains most appeal. Its position is not instantly obvious, for a row of modern houses has been built in front of it, on former railway land along Mill Road. Only when you take a footpath to Scratby do you chance upon it, converted into a house but in an overgrown and melancholy state. Great Ormesby was once a recommended alighting point for skaters. In severe winters, when the Broads froze over, the M&GN offered special cheap tickets from Yarmouth.

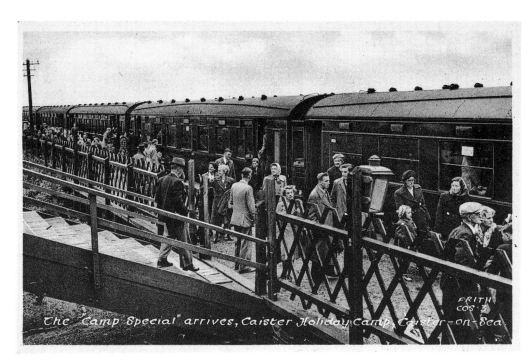

The "Camp Special" arrives, Caister Holiday Camp, Caister-on-Sea

**"CAMP SPECIAL" AT CAISTER CAMP HALT**

Not everyone looks delighted to have reached their holiday destinaton - perhaps retrieving luggage before the train pulled out was a more pressing concern! To judge by the clothes this Frith card probably dates from just after the Second World War. Camp Specials called at Potter Heigham and Hemsby as well, and normally ran on Saturdays. Caister Camp was the only one of the 1933 halts to have a normal-height platform. Traces of it can even today be spotted in the undergrowth.

CAISTER CAMP HALT

### *TANTIVY* RAILCAR NEAR CAISTER CAMP HALT

This six-cylinder steam railcar, built by Sentinel-Cammell and named *Tantivy*, was hired from the LNER to work the 1933 'new halts' service. The photograph is said to have been taken on a special trip just before the service began in earnest; but surely this crowd didn't all get on board? The railcar proved popular, but it only seated 48 and was expensive to run, so in succeeding years the halts were served by a locomotive and coaches - but everyone still called it *The Tantivy!*

BEACH ROAD AND RAILWAY STATION, CAISTER-ON-SEA.

**CAISTER-ON-SEA STATION**

"This is the West side of the Station. You can see the gates I have to open", runs the 1909 message on the reverse. Outward traffic from Caister once included considerable quantities of narcissi and daffodils from the Edmonds family's nurseries. The station acquired local fame for its hand-drawn posters, the work of the artistic porter Kerrison. Although the former almshouses in the centre of this view still stand, the station (visible to their left at the end of the short road) has been replaced by a row of houses. The crossing gates too have gone; the position occupied by the right-hand pair is now a car park entrance.

**YARMOUTH BEACH STATION**

When the young William Marriott first arrived here in 1881 he saw one short platform, a rudimentary building and a derelict windmill, all enclosed by a tumbledown fence! This view of about fifty years later shows an enlarged station which could handle thousands of holidaymakers at peak periods - in fact the 330-yard Platform 3 on the left was the M&GN's longest. The site was given over to motor coaches in 1962, but a few relics of the station were subsequently preserved by the roadside.

**STAFF AT YARMOUTH BEACH**

Stationmaster Albert Coe and his staff - two of them looking very junior! - pose for a group photograph. Fortunately someone had the foresight to put a caption and date on the tin tray!

**C CLASS 4-4-0 AT YARMOUTH BEACH SHED**

From the Yarmouth Beach platforms there was an excellent view of the goings-on in the goods yard and loco shed. As a result Wellesley Road residents found the backs of their guest-houses appearing in many photographs! Here C class no. 055 (plain no. 55 before renumbering by the LNER) stands outside the shed. Only the nearer half of the arch-roofed building served as the running shed; wagon sheets were made and repaired in the other half. Ten or eleven engines was the normal allocation here, but this would be increased in the summer.

**TRAIN CREW AT YARMOUTH BEACH**

About to leave Yarmouth with a holiday camp train in 1935 are (l to r) Fireman Walsh, Guard Youngman and Driver Thompson. No. 20 was one of the three A class 4-4-2 tanks built at Melton Constable. It is seen here after its side tanks had been tapered to improve visibility from the cab and reduce water surge (pages 81 and 99 show the original style of tank).

## 4. THE COASTAL ROUTE SOUTH FROM YARMOUTH

The direct route between Yarmouth and Lowestoft was opened in 1903 by the Norfolk & Suffolk Committee which belonged jointly to the M&GN and the GER. Trains served the former's Beach and the latter's South Town stations in Yarmouth, but after BR shut Breydon Viaduct in 1953 they could only go to South Town. Services eventually finished in 1970. In Gorleston the new Link Road will soon open along its course. At the time these postcards were issued trains crossed into Suffolk after Gorleston Links Halt; today the county boundary lies two miles further south.

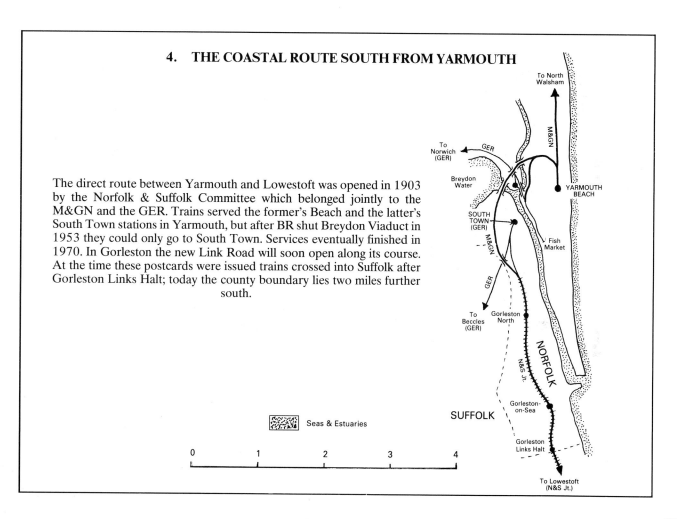

YARMOUTH FROM THE AIR. BREYDON SWING BRIDGE                    COPYRIGHT 1

### BREYDON VIADUCT

This five-span viaduct over Breydon Water had a working life of only fifty years. The position illustrated was its usual one as shipping had priority over trains. In a strong wind it could take ten minutes to open or close, whereas the 1986 road bridge on the same site lifts in just 90 seconds to let ships through. The viaduct was single-track on an otherwise double-track line, and had a signal-box at each end (the South box is at the far right) until the signalling was modernised in 1928. To the left is the mouth of the Bure which the railway also crossed as it looped north of the town from Beach station, and just visible at the top right is the GER's South Town terminus.

**GORLESTON-ON-SEA STATION**

The Great Eastern was responsible for building the line and so the intermediate stations had a GER feel to them. Compounding the effect in this view of Gorleston-on-sea station is the GER local working to Lowestoft. The station was set below the Lowestoft Road entrance and long covered walkways led down to the platforms. Like the other intermediate stations it became an unstaffed halt in 1966 and was very run down when closure came. At the time of writing the landscape has been devastated in preparation for Gorleston's new road scheme.

THE BUNGALOW ESTATE. GORLESTON.

NO.

**RAILCAR APPROACHING GORLESTON LINKS HALT**

Along the skyline comes the slightly blurred but recognizable shape of a Clayton steam railcar. The LNER bought five in 1928; they could run at 45 mph and were named after old mail coaches such as *Bang Up* and *Transit*. None of them lasted ten years in service. Just out of sight behind the hedge on the right were the windswept platforms of Gorleston Links Halt, opened for golfers in 1914. This scene has been totally transformed. Embankment, bridge and hedge have gone, and so has this bungalow, once a post office on the corner of Warren Road and Links Road. New housing has covered the whole area.

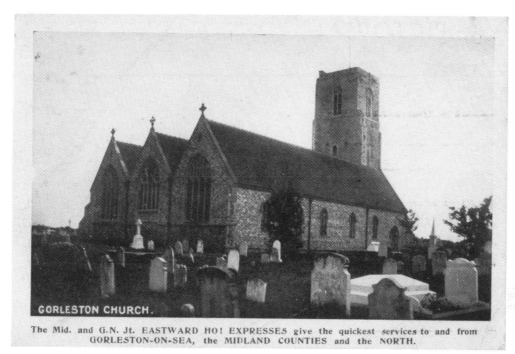

GORLESTON CHURCH.

The Mid. and G.N. Jt. EASTWARD HO! EXPRESSES give the quickest services to and from GORLESTON-ON-SEA, the MIDLAND COUNTIES and the NORTH.

## M&GN ADVERTISEMENT POSTCARD

Commercial postcards issued by the M&GN are particularly hard to come by. This survivor was posted in 1907 when you could catch a through train to Gorleston from Birmingham, Leeds or Manchester. Of all the scenes which the railway could have used to entice holidaymakers to the town, St. Andrew's church (which, apart from a new parish hall beside it, has changed little) and its graveyard seems an unlikely one.

**GER ADVERTISEMENT POSTCARD**

Perhaps of a more traditional appeal is this GER postcard announcing the 'new Coast Railway.' It was sent from Liverpool Street station in 1905 to advise a Wisbech lady that the lost property office could find no trace of her missing article. Maybe the sight of a steamer passing Gorleston's south pier on its way into harbour gave her some small consolation!

# 5. THE NORWICH CITY LINE

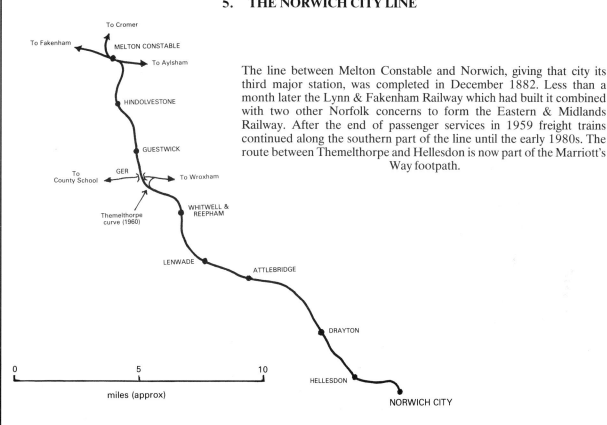

The line between Melton Constable and Norwich, giving that city its third major station, was completed in December 1882. Less than a month later the Lynn & Fakenham Railway which had built it combined with two other Norfolk concerns to form the Eastern & Midlands Railway. After the end of passenger services in 1959 freight trains continued along the southern part of the line until the early 1980s. The route between Themelthorpe and Hellesdon is now part of the Marriott's Way footpath.

The Station Hindolveston

**HINDOLVESTONE STATION**

An excellent detailed view of the pleasing pavilion-style building at Hindolvestone (unlike everyone else, the M&GN always insisted on the final "e"). Apart from the terminus every station on the Norwich line had this design of building. How many people, one wonders, were inspired by the Furness Railway's 'English Lakes' poster to undertake the 290-mile journey to Coniston or Windermere? Since closure sympathetic conversion of this station to a house has retained many features, while one of its slatted platform seats, the enamelled 'Hindolvestone' plate still in place, adorns a Norwich enthusiast's garden.

**TRAIN AT GUESTWICK STATION**

As 4-4-0 no.18 approaches with a train for Norwich, the Guestwick signalman seems in danger of forgetting to exchange tablets with the loco crew! Here, as elsewhere, automatic tablet exchanging equipment was introduced in 1906-7. The white diamond on the signal-box — more examples can be seen on other pages — indicated that the signalling system was functioning correctly. Turned over to show the black side, it was a sign for train crews to get the next station to summon assistance.

MIDLAND & G<sup>T</sup> NORTHERN GOODS COLLISION GUESTWICK Oct-31-08

**AFTERMATH OF A 1908 COLLISION AT GUESTWICK**

What a good Sunday's entertainment for these Guestwick folk! The previous evening two goods trains had collided in fog. People four miles away at Reepham claimed to have heard the impact. Both engine crews were fortunate to escape serious injury, but not so the goods wagons and their contents, which included fragile organ parts from the Norwich organ builders Norman & Beard, and a consignment of boots and shoes. A breakdown gang supervised by Mr. Marriott (standing by the crane, in a bowler hat) managed to clear the line on the Sunday ready for the trains to start running again on Monday.

Whitwell Station M & G.N.R.

**TRAIN AT WHITWELL AND REEPHAM STATION**

No.76, a 4-4-0 built in 1899 by Beyer Peacock & Co., stands with its cylinder cocks open at the northbound platform before attacking the 1 in 100 climb towards Themelthorpe. The steps in the right foreground led down the embankment to the road and were a useful short cut for Whitwell passengers. The footbridge was later dismantled and re-used at Gorleston-on-Sea. Those exploring Marriott's Way will find this one of the most evocative spots. Both platforms remain, though well overgrown, and young trees have camouflaged the derelict station building.

**LENWADE STATION**

A mid-1920s view of the station from the east. The three-siding goods yard (a petrol depot today) lies the other side of the station and its point rodding can be seen in the foreground. In 1957 Anglian Building Products, whose factory lay between Lenwade and Attlebridge, began despatching trainloads of concrete products such as bridge trusses and panels for prefabricated council flats. Before they could reach Norwich and their ultimate destination, often London, these huge loads had first to travel via Sheringham and North Walsham; but in 1960 the new Themelthorpe curve, a 500-yard link between the M&GN and the ex-GER Wroxham - County School branch, shortened their journey by almost twenty miles.

**LENWADE STATION APPROACH**

At first Lenwade signal-box was the Norwich side (i.e. to the right) of the station building, but when this and the previous card were issued it had been re-located on a new concrete base next to the level crossing. This was where the line crossed Porter's Lane, which leads from the Norwich - Fakenham road to Great Witchingham Hall. It was once planned to build a branch from here to East Dereham, but parliamentary approval was not forthcoming. The signal-box was demolished in 1974. The station building and the crossing gate shown here have survived, although both are in a neglected state.

The Station, Attlebridge.

Copyright
ATBG. 4.

### ATTLEBRIDGE STATION

An early Raphael Tuck coloured card taken from the goods yard and showing the station walls decorated with a mix of LMS and LNER posters. The ground frame on the left controlled the crossing and the sidings. Attlebridge station was fairly isolated when it opened, although recent years have seen development creep nearer. The station itself has become a house. There are modern windows on the ground floor and dormers jutting from the roof but the shaped bargeboards remain to give away the building's origin.

*Wishing you the good old wish for a very happy Xmas & Prosperous new Year*

**ATTLEBRIDGE GOODS YARD**

An unusual subject for a postcard, but the sender seems happy to use it for seasonal greetings! Again the station name is spelt out in stones, this time with the added adornment of a rose bed. The milepost shows that it is 44 miles from South Lynn. In the sidings are wagons belonging to coal merchants Fosdick of Ipswich and Bessey & Palmer of Yarmouth, the Lancashire, Derbyshire & East Coast Railway (swallowed up years before this card was posted in 1924!) and the M&GN's joint proprietors. As this land is today in private hands Marriott's Way veers away from the trackbed and runs along the fence by the field of drying hay before resuming its railway course to Drayton.

DRAYTON (FOR) COSTESSEY.

**TRAINS PASSING AT DRAYTON**

The only passing loops on the Norwich line were here and at Whitwell & Reepham. On the right a DA class 0-6-0 takes a mixed freight out of Norwich, while on the down train the last vehicle is an ex-GNR brake third. The running lines have been relaid with bullhead rail, but not the sidings where old flat-bottomed rail can still be seen. The white bracing post in the foreground helped to stabilise a tall signal just out of picture. As the caption indicates, the station was known for most of its life as Drayton for Costessey, but by the end BR timetables made do with Drayton.

DRAYTON STATION. *(Hall's Series.)* J 1365.

## GOODS TRAIN AT DRAYTON

At first glance working 'wrong line', this short train of open wagons headed by 4-4-0 no.32 may be waiting in the loop for an up passenger train to pass through. A new use was found for the footbridge, like Whitwell's, after the station closed; it was shifted just a quarter-of-a-mile to make it safer for pedestrians to cross the railway beside the A1067 road. The wooden sleepers from the Norwich - Drayton section, about eleven thousand in all, were piled up in Drayton yard and auctioned off there in 1973. The whole site has now become Drayton Industrial Estate.

HELLESDON STATION NR NORWICH

**HELLESDON STATION**

Given the rural location (only in recent years has New Costessey expanded towards the course of the line) it is surprising that an enlarged version of the standard station building was chosen for this site. This view of the station from the Marlpit Lane bridge shows foliage in abundance, and neatly sculptured around the doorway and platform seat. Hellesdon closed in 1952, some years before the line as a whole; the area is now a car park for walkers setting off along Marriott's Way.

TO GREET YOU RIGHT HEARTILY

THE DOLPHIN FERRY, BACK RIVER, NORWICH

**A—FRAME BRIDGE, NORWICH**

Three of these distinctive girder bridges, often called 'A-frame', carried the railway over the river Wensum between Drayton and Norwich (the one near Drayton is the sole survivor today). The bridge illustrated here was just up the line from Norwich City station; it had girders 5 ft. deep and a 70 ft. span. The ferry took its name from the nearby Dolphin Inn. It provided a short cut across the Back River (the old name for the Wensum above New Mills) between Drayton Road and Heigham Street. Norwich Corporation made the ferry redundant in 1909 when it opened the Dolphin footbridge over both the river and the railway.

Midland and Great Northern (City) Station, Norwich.

**NORWICH CITY STATION**

This grand terminus was built next to the river Wensum and half-a-mile north-west of the city centre. Its red brick facade was broken by pilasters of yellow brick, each capped so as to resemble carved stone. There were two floors each side of the main entrance and three in the left-hand 'tower' which included the stationmaster's accommodation. Through the arch lay two long canopied platforms, but the carriageway between them was open to the elements. The station was wrecked by enemy bombing in 1942 and a small prefabricated building put up in its place. This in turn was demolished in 1971 and all vestiges of the railway have disappeared beneath a trading estate and the Norwich inner ring road.

**WAITING ROOM AT NORWICH CITY STATION**

Interior views of M&GN buildings are quite rare, so we are fortunate to have this picture of the waiting room at the terminus. In the style of the period there is a dado rail separating the art nouveau wallpaper from the embossed paper below, and the fireplace with its tiled insert has the letters M&GN cast into it. The lady attendant has made it seem even more like an Edwardian drawing-room by surrounding the mirror with photographs of the royal family.

**PARCELS CARMEN AT NORWICH CITY STATION**

A superb line-up of carmen and their vehicles at the station entrance — but who are the pair of 'toffs' on the left? The importance of horses to the railway companies is sometimes overlooked; most had more horses than locomotives. Parcels carmen and draymen on the M&GN received 16/- per week, rising to 18/- in the third year. This put them ahead of porters but below shunters or signalmen.

# 6.  TO SHERINGHAM AND CROMER

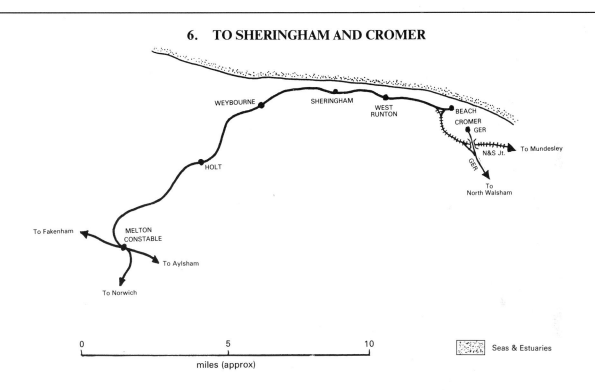

WEYBOURNE

SHERINGHAM

WEST
RUNTON

BEACH

CROMER
GER

N&S Jt.    To Mundesley

GER

To
North Walsham

HOLT

To Fakenham

MELTON
CONSTABLE

To Aylsham

To Norwich

0                5                10

miles (approx)

Seas & Estuaries

The undulating route from Melton Constable to these north Norfolk resorts (ending the GER's monopoly at Cromer) was completed by the Eastern & Midlands Railway in 1887. It managed to escape the 1959 closure, but five years later passenger services from Norwich Thorpe were cut back to Sheringham. The North Norfolk Railway's preserved trains now run from Sheringham to a new station east of Holt.

**BRININGHAM SIGNAL-BOX**

Trains leaving Melton Constable in three of the four directions — the exception was the Norwich branch — ran along a double track to begin with. Going towards Cromer, the 13-lever box at Briningham Single Line Junction marked the transition to single track. M&GN signal-boxes had their structural timbers painted tan and their weatherboarding a lighter stone colour. Window frames were white. The wooden platform seen here by the box steps was for facilitating tablet exchange. Briningham box remained open until services ended but was removed a few years later. Subsequent housing development has destroyed most traces of the line at this point.

Holt Railway Station. J 3529. (*Basham's Series*).

## HOLT STATION

The Eastern & Midlands Company was not financially strong, and it was a very basic railway which struggled into Holt in 1884. This remained the terminus for nearly three years while money was sought for the onward push to Cromer. Holt's main building, seen on the right in this early 1920s card (and erected in place of the original wooden hut) was burnt down in 1926. A replacement was erected using 'Marriott patent' concrete blocks. The railway ran just south of the town and in 1981-2 a much-needed Holt by-pass was built along its course. Only the tall granary was left standing; the signal-box had previously been removed to further active service at the North Norfolk Railway's Weybourne station.

THE STATION, WEYBOURNE  J & S 563

**WEYBOURNE STATION**

There were originally no plans for a station here but in 1901 residents persuaded the railway to build one. This Jarrold view shows the west end of the main building. The stationmaster's house is in the centre of the picture and Weybourne village three-quarters-of-a-mile across the fields to the north. Weybourne signal-box enjoyed a magnificent view of North Sea shipping, and signalmen used to keep a telescope at hand! The station is now in the care of the North Norfolk Railway whose engineering workshops occupy the old yard.

**UP EXPRESS NEAR WEYBOURNE**

The spirit of the Joint! A gleaming 4-4-0, resplendent in 'golden gorse' livery, rushes through the countryside near Weybourne with an express from Cromer. The caption on the reverse of this card identifies the train as the 3.20 pm express. This train reached Melton Constable at 3.58 pm and was attached to portions from Lowestoft and Norwich City. Leicester was reached at 7 pm and Birmingham New Street an hour later.

S 6919　　　　GOLF CLUB & CADDY HOUSE SHERINGHAM.

## LEVEL CROSSING AT SHERINGHAM GOLF CLUB

Contestants in the prestigious golf championships staged at Sheringham need extra concentration coming in, as the last holes overlook the North Norfolk Railway where during the summer as many as eighteen trains can run by each day. This c.1925 view looks across the course towards the sea. Since then the railway crossing over Sweetbriar Lane has lost its gates and the old club house on the left has been converted into a private house.

**CLAUD HAMILTON 4-4-0 AT SHERINGHAM**

This GER Claud Hamilton 4-4-0 is attracting a lot of attention. The Great Eastern was allowed into Sheringham from 1906 and its Liverpool Street expresses competed with the M&GN's King's Cross services. After the LNER's takeover of locomotives on the M&GN in 1936, 'Clauds' could be found all over the Joint. In the foreground the small tumbler ground signal for trains leaving the siding is of interest. Sheringham station is now the North Norfolk Railway's headquarters. The footbridge and up side buildings have gone and the goods yard has become a car park. BR trains have been banished to a bare platform 200 yards nearer Norwich so that cars no longer get held up at the Station Road gates.

**ACCIDENT AT SHERINGHAM**

The M&GN used to complain about the GER making more use of Sheringham station than they had a right to; so no doubt they were livid when they saw what this GER carriage had done to their up platform offices! The carriage is probably one of those which formed the Sheringham portion of the Norfolk Coast Express, inaugurated in 1907, but neither the exact date of the incident nor its cause has been traced. Despite this and a number of other mishaps, it was the Joint's proud boast that during its existence not one passenger was killed on its lines.

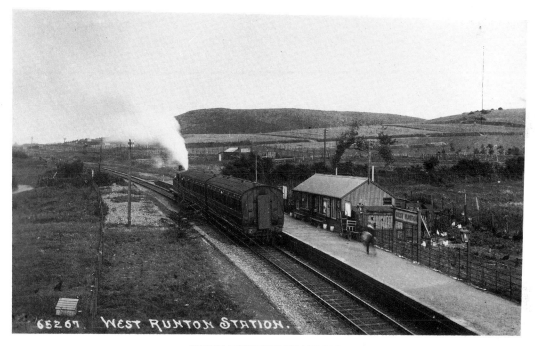

65267. WEST RUNTON STATION.

**WEST RUNTON STATION**

A GER 2-4-2 tank engine and local train have just stopped, and a solitary passenger walks away past the chickens scratching about. West Runton boasted not a single siding yet it still warranted its own stationmaster. His office, along with a booking hall and small waiting room, was housed in the corrugated iron hut, and one of his duties was to hoist a red flag when passengers wished to join a train on a 'conditional' stop. The station was manned until 1967. West Runton and Cromer are the only ex-M&GN stations in Norfolk where British Rail trains still call.

Cromer Beach Station.

**CROMER BEACH STATION**

The E&M's Cromer Beach terminus opened in June 1887. There were four daily arrivals from London and three departures, and passengers were invited to patronize the 'commodious refreshment and dining rooms' in the attractive mock-Tudor building. Here no.26, an A class 4-4-0, is ready to leave from Platform 2 with a train of mixed ex-GNR and ex-E&M vehicles. Across the platform stands a rake of MR express stock. The station became simply 'Cromer' in 1969 (the E&M's 'Beach' had been there to emphasize the GER's inconvenient position) and today there are just two tracks, one each side of the platform. Dwarfing the station is a new supermarket.

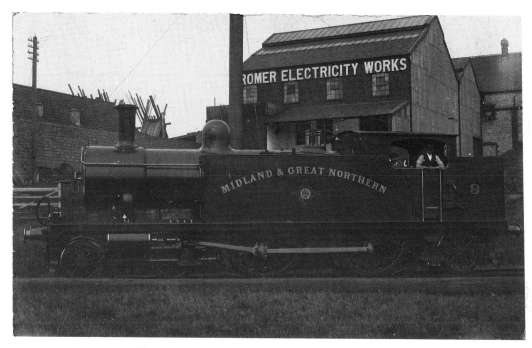

**A CLASS TANK LOCOMOTIVE AT CROMER BEACH**

No.9 was the last of the three A class 4-4-2 tank engines to be built. It first saw service in 1910. What a grand sight it makes standing in Cromer's loco siding with its tanks displaying the company's name in gold lettering and its heraldic device. No.9 ran until 1944. Cromer UDC's electricity works was just north of the station. The gates on the left of the picture closed across the private siding which the works shared with the council depot next door.

# 7. THE MUNDESLEY LINE

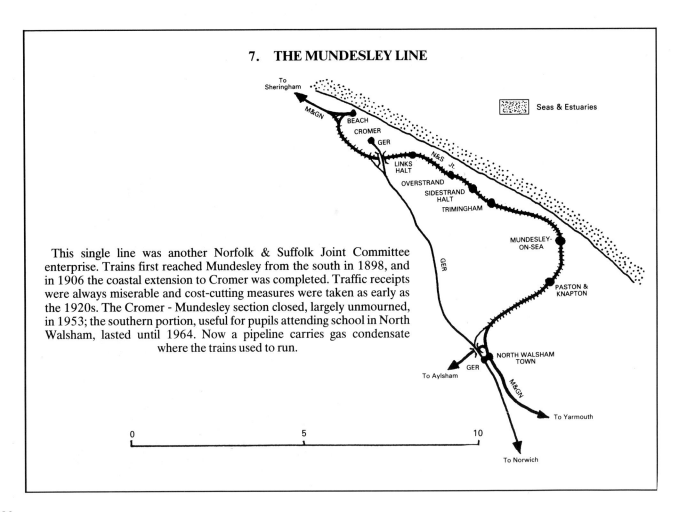

This single line was another Norfolk & Suffolk Joint Committee enterprise. Trains first reached Mundesley from the south in 1898, and in 1906 the coastal extension to Cromer was completed. Traffic receipts were always miserable and cost-cutting measures were taken as early as the 1920s. The Cromer - Mundesley section closed, largely unmourned, in 1953; the southern portion, useful for pupils attending school in North Walsham, lasted until 1964. Now a pipeline carries gas condensate where the trains used to run.

## RUNTON WEST JUNCTION SIGNAL-BOX

At this junction the Cromer and Mundesley lines diverged. The signal-box was equipped with a Tyer's No.1 tablet machine and a double-line block instrument. The prominent board below the signalman warned enginemen of the presence of self-acting catch points near the junction. Three junctions — this one, Runton East and Newstead Lane — formed the 'Runton triangle'. Working their boxes was so intricate that a large plywood model of the layout, complete with signals and block instruments, was used to help signalmen master the procedures. All three boxes were taken out of use in 1963 following track and signalling alterations.

44548   THE VIADUCTS, EAST RUNTON

## EAST RUNTON VIADUCTS

Just a quarter-of-a-mile from Runton West box the Cromer (rear) and Mundesley (front) lines crossed Green's Lane. The front viaduct, on a curve as well as inclined at 1 in 80, has been out of use since 1960; trains from Norwich use the triangle's east side to reach Cromer after which, having reversed, they travel along the rear viaduct to get to Sheringham.

**RELAYING TRACK AT ROUGHTON ROAD JUNCTION**

The Cromer - Mundesley - North Walsham line was single track but here where the gangers are at work it was doubled in order to ease traffic working at Roughton Road Junction. This was where the line was joined by the short spur (behind the box) built to connect the GER's main line with the Mundesley line and to give the GER access, via Runton West Curve, to Sheringham. The spur is still part of BR's Norwich - Sheringham line. The tablet catching posts are manual ones because GER engines working the Mundesley route were not fitted with automatic exchange apparatus. The signal-box with its appealing half-hipped roof closed in 1961 and was demolished some years later.

OVERSTRAND STATION.

## OVERSTRAND STATION

Much of the line at Overstrand was on an embankment, and to reach the long island platform you had to enter the white-tiled subway in the centre of this view and walk up the long ramp with its roof of frosted glass. As part of the 1920s economy drive the signal-box was closed and the passing loop dispensed with, so that track remained only on the seaward side, i.e. where the train is standing. Despite this there was still a through service from London right up to the line's closure in 1953; the 'Broadsman' left Liverpool Street at 3.30 pm and drew in to Overstrand at 6.51 pm.

**SIDESTRAND HALT**

The Norfolk & Suffolk Committee was keen to capture whatever pockets of trade it might have overlooked, so after the line had been open for some years two extra halts were built: Cromer Links (opened in July 1923) and this one at Sidestrand (May 1936). It was to be found down an inconspicuous footpath from the Overstrand - Trimingham coast road. Its short cinder-topped platform was equipped with the basic necessities of nameboard, timetables and lamps.

Trimingham Station, Norfolk.

**TRIMINGHAM STATION**

Here and at Overstrand the stations were built by C. A. Sadler of Sheringham, and both buildings were of the same brick and terracotta design, with the corrugated iron roof extending over the canopy. This view shows the station's south end, where the booking hall was in a corridor behind the cyclists. As at Overstrand the signal-box and passing loop were later removed, and so for the latter half of its life this side of the platform saw no trains at all. The station site has since been used for housing.

**MUNDESLEY-ON-SEA STATION**

To cater for the holiday crowds — who never materialised — Mundesley boasted a spacious station with four platforms. Until 1930 it also had two signal-boxes and its own engine shed. The much-admired station building was the work of North Walsham builders Cornish & Gaymer. It was topped with a fine clock tower and weathervane, and a wall-mounted bell signalled the approach of a train. In the picture a GER service has arrived from North Walsham. Less than a year after the trains ceased in 1964, the station and twelve acres of railway land fetched £12,150 at auction; the area is now covered with bungalows.

**PASTON & KNAPTON STATION**

Looking more like a rectory or guest house than a railway station, Paston & Knapton was never busy. In its early years less than ten passengers a day caught a train here. Through the gate to the left of the main entrance a footpath led over the line to Knapton village, while the pair of gates where the bicycle is leaning were the way in to the two-siding goods yard.

By the time closure came this handsome building had been downgraded to an unstaffed halt. It is now a private house.

"666" Conference Train. derailed. N.Walsham

## DERAILMENT AT NORTH WALSHAM

This calamity occured on the crossover at the Cromer end of GER's North Walsham station whose platform canopies may be seen in the background. It would be some time before GER 2-4-2T no.666 managed to complete its journey to the destination clipped to its bunker, as it had come well and truly off the rails. Each partner in the Norfolk & Suffolk Committee ran its own trains along the branch, and the conference delegates were probably ushered smartly across to the M&GN station to continue their journey.

**M&GN HERALDIC DEVICE**

The device, inherited from the Eastern & Midlands Railway, was carried by some locomotives. Three of its quarters represented places in Norfolk: (clockwise, from top right) Norwich, King's Lynn and Yarmouth. The top left-hand quarter represented the Bishop and See of Peterborough.

## 8. LOCOMOTIVES

As befitted a railway with such a complex family tree, the M&GN's locomotive stock came from several sources, including both parent companies, a Cornish mineral line — and of course Melton Works itself. When LNER took over in 1936, every joint engine was at least twenty-seven years old, and the old stalwarts shown on the following pages were steadily consigned to the scrap line.

**0-6-0ST No.16A**

One of the pair of engines which were delivered to the Great Yarmouth & Stalham Railway in 1877 by Fox, Walker & Co. of Bristol, who specialised in small saddle tanks. After arriving at Yarmouth Vauxhall, they were pulled by horses through the streets to their destination. No.16A (originally No.16 and named *Stalham*) became the works shunter at Melton Constable where it was photographed in June 1929. Nicknamed 'Black Bess' it completed sixty years' service before withdrawal.

**A CLASS 4-4-0 NO.25**

The Eastern & Midlands Railway's principal passenger locomotives were these outside-cylinder 4-4-0s manufactured at the Gorton Foundry of Beyer Peacock & Co. The maker's name can be seen in brass around the leading splasher, and the engines were known as 'Peacocks'. No.25, seen here at Melton Constable, has an elaborately decked-out front end. The Cromer extension opened on 16th June 1887, five days before Queen Victoria's golden jubilee, so the locomotive may have been about to haul a train in celebration of one or both of these events.

**C CLASS 4-4-0 No.1**

When the M&GN was formed in 1893, locomotives and rolling stock were the Midland Railway's responsibility; thus the C class 4-4-0s which began arriving the following year were a standard Midland design. Here no.1, given the prefix '0' by the LNER, simmers quietly inside Norwich engine shed. A sister engine, no.047, was severely damaged in this shed during a 1942 air raid.

S 8427      M. & G. N. JT. RLY. EXPRESS PASSENGER ENGINE.

**C CLASS 4-4-0 No.53**

Several of the class were rebuilt with a larger boiler and Belpaire firebox. The first, in 1910, was no.53, portrayed here in the 'works grey' finish which was usual for official photographs. Comparison with no.1 on the previous page shows that its splashers have been altered to a plain design. The slot was later restored, though, to make it easier to lubricate the coupling rods when they were at '12 o'clock'.

**MR CLASS 0-6-0T No.97**

The nine MR (Melton rebuild) class engines were usually to be found on shunting and station pilot duties. This 1934 view shows no.97 shunting behind Yarmouth's Wellesley Road. Though officially described as rebuilt by virtue of re-using a few parts from older engines, the MR class were pretty well built from scratch. In 1943 the 40-year-old no.97 was the first to be withdrawn, but three of the class, classified J93 by the LNER, lasted into the British Railways era.

**Da CLASS 0-6-0 LOCOMOTIVE**

The Joint had a 28-strong fleet of 0-6-0 freight engines. The first sixteen were of a standard Midland Railway design, but the twelve delivered in 1900, an example of which appears here, were originally ordered by the GNR for their own line and then diverted to the M&GN which at the time was short of freight engines. The 'Yorkies' as they were known usually worked west of King's Lynn, but this one has strayed as far as Yarmouth. On its leading splasher is the familiar diamond-shaped worksplate of its Glasgow builders, Dubs & Co.

**A CLASS 4-4-2T No.41**

Yarmouth's signal gantry and water tanks provide the backdrop for a striking study of No.41. This was the first of the eventual class of three engines to emerge from Melton Works, in 1904; they were officially rebuilds but like the 0-6-0Ts they were to all intents and purposes new engines. They often worked along the coast to Lowestoft or up to Potter Heigham, and a regular turn at one time was the Saturday morning market train from Melton Constable to Norwich. All three were withdrawn during the Second World War.

**BOUNDARY POST**

Formed from a length of steel rail and embedded several feet in the ground, these posts marked the boundary of the Committee's land. One or two may still be discovered in situ today.

## 9.   MISCELLANY

The following cards illustrate some other aspects of life on the Joint.

## BOOKSTALL AT HOLT STATION

Railway bookstalls were often no more than a lockable cabinet and a trestle table, such as this arrangement on the wooden platform at Holt. A view of Melton Constable station is among the postcards displayed on the rack. The railway companies' posters are noteworthy: the M&GN illustrating the pleasures of the seaside just down the line, and the Midland, noted as a champion of the third-class passenger, claiming to be 'the best route for comfort'. Such pictorial posters are today prized by railwayana collectors and art lovers alike.

**UNLOADING RAILS**

One of a railway's most awkward loads was its own rails! This view taken near Caister in 1931 shows a permanent way gang in the process of unloading the 60-foot lengths. The eight men would lever each rail to the edge of the bolster wagons and lower it down special ramps which were themselves formed from rail. New sleepers would normally have been delivered by an earlier train and stacked at intervals along the track.

**TRACK GANG'S HUTS**

Foreman Mr. Strangleman (right), previously seen on page 21, and one of his gang stand surrounded by sleepers, rails and the tools of their trade in this view which dates from around 1920. In those pre-mechanization days track maintenance was an arduous task requiring men who were adept with tools as diverse as hammers, shovels, 'Jim crow' rail benders and scythes. Was the chalked notice 'No Admittance After Ten' a comment on timekeeping or the hut's capacity?

## M&GN RAILWAYMAN

This young M&GN employee, porter or clerk maybe, looks slightly resentful at being asked to pose in uniform. Until the mid-1920s when blue cloth became the norm, the M&GN uniform consisted of green corduroy jacket, waistcoat and trousers. A replacement set was issued annually, but without buttons; they had to be transferred from the old uniform. The peaked cap was made of green cloth and its 'MID & GN' badge was formed from a strip of brass.

## M&GN NORWICH CITY OFFICE

To compensate for its station being some way away from the commercial heart of a city, a railway company would often open a centrally-sited office. (Neighbouring shopkeepers were then apt to complain about the congestion caused by so many goods deliveries!). The M&GN's Norwich office with its elegant facade of brick, tile and stone was at No.16 Haymarket. The GER had an office just yards away at No.24.

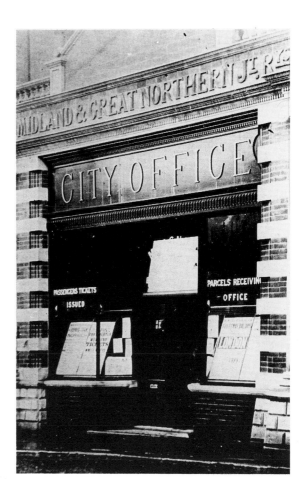

# ACKNOWLEDGEMENTS

Pride of place has to go to the M&GN Circle*. Since 1959 it has assiduously published documents, reminiscences and illustrations of the Joint, and its monthly Bulletin has proved an invaluable source of material; thanks are due to editor Mick Clark. The Circle's archivist, Nigel Digby, provided information on architecture and rolling stock, and the following members were also helpful: Richard Adderson, Deryck Featherstone, Sibyl Kirk, Raymond Meek, Peter Starling and Phyllis Youngman. The staff of Norwich City Library's Local Studies Department shed light on some puzzles, as did Neil Storey of North Walsham.

Other useful printed sources included:

R. H. Clark - *A Short History of the M&GN* (Goose & Son, 1967)
D. I. Gordon - *A Regional History of the Railways of Great Britain*
     *Vol. 5: Eastern Counties* (David & Charles, 1968)
R. S. Joby - *The Norfolk & Suffolk Joint Railways Committee* (Klofron, 1975)
A. J. Wrottesley - *The Midland and Great Northern Joint Railway* (David & Charles, 1970)

Postcards used in the book are from Philip Standley's collection apart from the following, for whose loan we are grateful: Mrs R. Bunn: pp.17, 21, 24, 36, 62, 66, 72, 79, 103; H. C. Casserley: p.93; Mr. Checkley: p.13; Mr. & Mrs. Colman: p.101; D. Cross: pp.6, 14, 43, 44, 51, 54, 85, 91; R. Fisher: pp.23, 95, 99; G. Gosling: p.96; I. Hurst: p.57; M&GN Circle: p.9 (source B. L. Ridgway, North Norfolk Railway and Anglia Television Ltd.), p.16 (source B. S. Willard), p.18 (source A. Attoe, photo by A. W. Coen), p.22 (source A. M. Wells), p.70 (source Mr. & Mrs. Leverett), p.105 (source B. L. Ridgway); M. Storey-Smith: pp.37, 45, 52, 75, 78, 87, 98, 102; Mrs. P. Youngman: pp.48, 74.

*The M&GN Circle welcomes new members. Enquiries should be addressed to:
G. L. Kenworthy, 16 Beverley Road, Brundall, Norwich, NR13 5QS.

S. B. Publications publish a wide range of local books illustrating East Anglia and other parts of the country in the series *A Portrait in Old Picture Postcards*.
For full details of current and forthcoming publications write (inc. S.A.E) to:
S. B. Publications, Unit 2, The Old Station Yard, Pipe Gate, Market Drayton, Shropshire TF9 4HY.